A Lord of the Rings Inspired Cookbook

Return of the Kitchen Wizard - Magical Middle-earth Desserts

By Mia Martin

Copyright 2024 Mia Martin.

License Notes

This is my least favorite part about writing books: the copyright. I can imagine this is your least favorite part as well, often even flipping right past this page. I don't blame you. Still, I am obligated to ask you to refrain from making any print or electronic reproductions, selling, republishing, or distributing this book in parts or as a whole unless you have express written consent from my team or me. You are not allowed to do so under any circumstance.

If reading this is annoying for you, imagine how annoying it must be for me to write it or even actually see it happen…It's not that I'm trying to be mean or bossy, but I worked very hard on this book, and not getting any credit for it is quite discouraging because many times, people who reproduce my books use my recipes in their own name or republish the book without mine! I've seen it all… So, if you're reading this, please don't infringe on the copyrights to my work.

Table of Contents

Introduction 5

1. Shelob's Sticky Bun 7

2. Precious Chocolate 10

3. Merry's Berry Cheese Cake 13

4. Bilbo's Banana Pudding 17

5. Frodo's Surprise 20

6. Prune Tree Cake 23

7. The Eye of Sauron 27

8. Lemon Ice 31

9. LOTR Pudding 34

10. Sweet Tater Cake 37

11. Sam and Rosie Chocolate Strawberries 41

12. Helm's Deep Bundt Cake 44

13. Lemon Butter 47

14. Lembas Biscuits 50

15. Aragorn's Gift 53

16. Bag End Blueberry Crepe 56

17. Gimli's Brownies 59

18. An Unexpected Cinnamon Cheesecake 62

19. Hadhafang Spears 66

20. Spiderweb Fondue 69

21. Middle Earth Coconut Balls 73

22. Sam's Squares 76

23. Gandalf's Coffee Cake 80

24. Lord of the Ring Cake 84

25. Rosie's Butter Pecan Cheesecake 88

26. Glazed Eye of Sauron 92

27. Frodo's Lemon Cakes 96

28. Weary Traveler Buns 100

29. Good Weather in the Shire Apple Bake 103

30. Travel Party Rice Pudding 106

31. Spider's Eyes Brownie 109

32. Elvish Nut Brittle 112

Author's Afterthoughts 115

Introduction

I wholeheartedly believe depicting cuisine should have a place in various creative mediums, films especially. Sentient beings cannot survive without nourishment — regardless whether they're embattled against orcs, nestled in ent boughs or captive to colossal arachnids. Indeed The Lord of the Rings incorporates many scenes where hobbits, dwarves and elves partake in victuals and libations alike.

Such interludes can certainly provide a source of comedy, like the hobbits' continual feasting or Gimli and Legolas's drinking game. Yet they also reveal the characters' fundamental humanity, while spotlighting the unlikely bonds forged between these quirky cohorts. When audiences watch motley crews breaking bread onscreen, the sense of camaraderie kindled in those moments sparks an affinity that transcends differences. After all, viewers too know the unifying simplicity of sharing a meal.

Please let me know if I should modify or add anything to this version! I aimed to keep the primary concepts while putting it in slightly different terms.

ssssssssssssssssssssss

1. Shelob's Sticky Bun

Shelob is a killer spider in the LOTR books who captures Frodo when Gollum lures him into her lair. These sticky buns won't limit your movement, but they will tantalize your taste buds.

Prep Time: 15 minutes

Serve: 4

List of Ingredients:

- 2 large eggs
- 4 oz of caster sugar
- 4 oz of softened butter
- 1 oz of golden syrup
- 3 oz of all-purpose flour
- 2 1/2 teaspoons of baking powder

sssssssssssssssssssssss

Methods:

a. Begin by preparing the sticky syrup for Shelob's Sticky Bun. Pour the golden syrup into a microwave-safe mixing bowl (34 oz capacity). Swirl the syrup around in the bowl to ensure it coats the bottom and sides evenly.

b. In a separate bowl, take your 2 large eggs, 4 oz of caster sugar, 4 oz of softened butter, 3 oz of all-purpose flour, and 2 1/2 teaspoons of baking powder. Mix these ingredients together thoroughly until you have a smooth and well-combined mixture.

c. Now, gently pour the flour mixture into the bowl containing the golden syrup. Ensure that it covers the syrup evenly.

d. Cover the mixing bowl with plastic wrap, making sure it's tightly sealed to prevent any steam from escaping.

e. Microwave the covered bowl on high for approximately 6 minutes. This will cook the mixture and create a delicious sponge cake.

f. Once done, carefully remove the bowl from the microwave. Be cautious as it will be hot. Allow the sponge cake to cool for about 5 minutes.

g. After the brief cooling period, transfer the Shelob's Sticky Bun from the mixing bowl to a suitable serving dish.

Did you know?

- Shelob, the giant spider from the Lord of the Rings, was a formidable and terrifying creature that guarded the pass of Cirith Ungol. This recipe's name pays homage to this iconic character from J.R.R. Tolkien's epic fantasy world.
- The golden syrup used in this recipe is reminiscent of the precious gold ring that plays a central role in the Lord of the Rings trilogy. Just as the ring is highly sought after, the golden syrup adds a touch of sweetness that makes this sticky bun so enticing.
- While making Shelob's Sticky Bun, take a moment to immerse yourself in the magical world of Middle-earth and enjoy a taste of the fantastical adventures that unfolded in Tolkien's masterpiece. This recipe brings a touch of the Shire to your kitchen, allowing you to experience a small part of the enchanting realm created by the beloved author.

2. Precious Chocolate

Perhaps Sauron's eye was looking for chocolate all along instead of the ring held by Frodo. Orange and chocolate are two flavors that complement each other perfectly.

Prep Time: 10 minutes

Serve: 20

List of Ingredients:

- 2 oz of pecans, chopped
- 13 oz of chocolate chips
- 14 oz of sweetened condensed milk
- ½ an oz of grated orange zest

ssssssssssssssssssssssss

Methods:

a. Start by lining an 8"x8" baking tin with parchment paper. This will make it easier to remove the chocolate later.

b. Next, take a microwavable bowl and add the chocolate and condensed milk. Heat this mixture in the microwave for 1-3 minutes, using 30-second intervals. After each interval, be sure to stir the mixture thoroughly until it is completely melted and smooth. This ensures a creamy texture for your chocolate.

c. Once the chocolate and condensed milk are perfectly blended, it's time to enhance the flavor. Add the pecans and the zest of an orange to the melted chocolate. Stir these ingredients in until they are well combined. This step adds a delightful crunch and a hint of citrusy freshness to your chocolate treat.

d. With your chocolate mixture now beautifully infused with pecans and orange zest, carefully pour it into the prepared baking tin. Ensure that the mixture is evenly distributed in the tin.

e. Place the baking tin in the refrigerator and allow it to chill for 2-3 hours. This cooling time will allow the chocolate to set and become firm.

f. After the chocolate has properly chilled, remove it from the refrigerator. Using a sharp knife, cut the chocolate into squares of your desired size. The parchment paper lining will make it easy to lift the chocolate out of the tin and cut it neatly.

Did you know?

- The term "Precious" in the recipe's name is a nod to Gollum's famous obsession with the "One Ring" in J.R.R. Tolkien's Lord of the Rings series. Just as Gollum referred to the ring as "my precious," this chocolate treat can become your own precious indulgence.
- The use of orange zest in the recipe adds a touch of brightness and complexity to the chocolate, much like the multifaceted characters and rich world-building found in Tolkien's epic fantasy novels.
- This recipe's careful attention to detail and precision in melting the chocolate mirrors the intricate storytelling and craftsmanship evident in Tolkien's works. Just as the author took great care in crafting his stories, this recipe emphasizes the importance of patience and precision to create a delectable chocolate delight.

3. Merry's Berry Cheese Cake

While cheesecake is not a food that would have shown up in Tolkien's books, I am sure the Hobbits would have enjoyed this dessert for a meal or two. Sprinkle some blueberries or grind them up and add sugar for blueberry sauce.

Prep Time: 10 minutes

Serve: 12

List of Ingredients:

Crust

- 1 oz of erythritol
- ½ teaspoon of vanilla extract
- 10 oz of almond flour
- 2 oz of butter

Filling

- 1 teaspoon of lemon zest
- ½ teaspoon of vanilla extract
- 2 oz of blueberries, fresh or frozen
- 20 oz of cream cheese
- 4 oz of crème fraîche
- 2 large eggs
- 1 egg yolk
- ½ an oz of erythritol

Methods:

Crust:

a. Begin by preheating your oven to 350 degrees Fahrenheit.
b. Take a 9" springform baking pan and coat it with cooking spray. Line the pan with parchment paper to ensure easy removal later.
c. In the baking pan, melt 2 oz of butter until it becomes fragrant and nutty. Remove the melted butter from the oven, and then add 10 oz of almond flour, 1 oz of erythritol, and ½ teaspoon of vanilla extract to the melted butter.
d. Knead this mixture into a dough, and then press it down evenly along the base of the pan to create the crust.
e. Bake the crust in the preheated oven for 8-10 minutes, or until it turns a beautiful golden brown. Once done, remove it from the oven and allow it to cool.

Filling:

a. In a large mixing bowl, combine the remaining ingredients from your list except for the blueberries. This includes 20 oz of cream cheese, 4 oz of crème fraîche, 2 large eggs, 1 egg yolk, ½ oz of erythritol, 1 teaspoon of lemon zest, and ½ teaspoon of vanilla extract. Mix these ingredients until you have a smooth and creamy filling.
b. Pour this delectable filling over the cooled crust in the baking pan, ensuring an even distribution.
c. Now, increase the oven temperature to 400 degrees Fahrenheit, and place the cheesecake back into the oven. Bake for 15 minutes.
d. After 15 minutes, reduce the oven temperature to 230 degrees Fahrenheit and continue baking for an additional 45-60 minutes. This gradual temperature change ensures that your cheesecake cooks evenly and maintains its creamy texture.

e. Once the baking is complete, turn off the oven and let the cheesecake cool inside the oven. This gradual cooling process helps prevent cracks on the surface.
f. After cooling in the oven, remove the cheesecake and let it chill in the refrigerator overnight. This extended chilling period allows the flavors to meld and the cheesecake to set perfectly.
g. When ready to serve, garnish your Merry's Berry Cheesecake with fresh or frozen blueberries, adding a burst of vibrant color and fruity flavor.

Did you know?

- Merry, one of the hobbits from the Lord of the Rings, is known for his adventurous spirit and love of good food. This cheesecake, bearing his name, is a tribute to his character and the warm, comforting flavors associated with the Shire.
- The concept of second breakfast, a beloved hobbit tradition, is reminiscent of the joy of indulging in dessert at any time of day. This cheesecake's creamy richness and berry topping would surely be a delightful choice for any hobbit's second breakfast.
- The gradual cooling process used in this recipe mirrors the patience and dedication displayed by the characters in the Lord of the Rings saga. Just as the fellowship embarked on a long and challenging journey, this cheesecake requires time and care to reach its full potential, resulting in a truly delightful treat for your taste buds.

4. Bilbo's Banana Pudding

Food wasn't just wrapped in banana leaves while travelling, but the bananas themselves would make an appearance in recipes. This pudding is decadent and delicious for any creature in Middle Earth.

Prep Time: 10 minutes

Serve: 2

List of Ingredients:

- 1 beaten egg
- 1 ripened mashed banana
- 3 oz of self-raising flour
- A good pinch of cinnamon
- 5 tablespoons of golden syrup
- 2 oz of butter
- 2 ½ oz of sugar
- 1 teaspoon of allspice

ssssssssssssssssssssssss

Methods:

a. To begin, take a bowl and your trusty electric mixer. Cream together the butter and sugar until the mixture becomes delightfully fluffy. This step ensures a rich and creamy base for your pudding.

b. Now, introduce the egg into the buttery goodness and mix it in until the ingredients are harmoniously blended. Once done, stir in the mashed banana until the mixture reaches a smooth consistency, infusing the dessert with that irresistible banana flavor.

c. It's time to add some depth of flavor and warmth to your pudding. Incorporate the flour, allspice, and cinnamon into the batter, and mix vigorously. These spices will infuse your dessert with a comforting and aromatic touch.

d. To create a visually appealing marbled effect, gently fold the syrup into the batter. This step not only adds sweetness but also gives your pudding an enticing swirl of flavors and colors.

e. Now, it's time to cook your creation to perfection. Place the batter into a microwave-safe container and cook it on high for approximately 5 minutes. Keep an eye on it to ensure it doesn't overflow.

f. After the cooking is complete, allow your Bilbo's Banana Pudding to cool slightly before serving. This short resting period allows the flavors to settle, making each spoonful a delectable experience.

Did you know?

- Bilbo Baggins, the adventurous hobbit from J.R.R. Tolkien's The Hobbit and The Lord of the Rings, was known for his unexpected journey and love of good food. This pudding bears his name as a nod to his epic adventures and his appreciation for hearty, comforting dishes.
- Hobbits in Tolkien's world are renowned for their culinary skills, and desserts like this banana pudding would undoubtedly be a cherished treat in the Shire. It reflects the cozy and indulgent nature of hobbit cuisine.
- Just as Bilbo's journey led to the discovery of the One Ring, this recipe invites you on a delightful culinary journey. The marbled appearance of the pudding represents the unexpected twists and turns in the epic tale of Middle-earth, where surprises and discoveries await at every corner.

5. Frodo's Surprise

This creamy concoction would have been an exotic treat for a Hobbit who was used to have heavier and thicker fare as a dessert. Add some berries or caramel sauce to sweeten it up even more.

Prep Time: 5 minutes

Serve: 2

List of Ingredients:

- ½ teaspoon of vanilla extract
- 1 oz of erythritol
- 2 eggs, separated into whites and yolks
- 10 oz of heavy whipping cream

sssssssssssssssssssssss

Methods:

a. Start by taking a large mixing bowl and focus on beating the egg yolks until they reach a delightful level of fluffiness. This step is crucial for achieving a smooth and creamy texture in your surprise dessert.

b. Now, let's move to a small saucepan. Combine the cream, vanilla, and sweetener in it, and set it on medium heat. Allow the mixture to come to a gentle boil, and keep a close eye on it. As it simmers, you'll notice it thickening gradually.

c. Once the mixture in the saucepan has thickened, it's time to make the next move. Reduce the heat to low, and with great care, pour the fluffy beaten egg yolks into the creamy concoction. Stir diligently to ensure a harmonious blend, and keep stirring as the mixture continues to thicken further.

d. With your mixture now beautifully combined, it's time to let it cool down. Place the saucepan in the refrigerator, allowing the mixture to chill and set. This step is crucial for the texture and consistency of Frodo's Surprise.

e. While your creamy base is cooling, shift your attention to the egg whites. Whisk them together until they reach a state of fluffiness that's akin to clouds. This fluffy texture will add a delightful lightness to your dessert.

f. Once your creamy base has chilled adequately, gently fold the fluffy egg whites into it. This careful blending adds an ethereal quality to the dessert, making it both creamy and airy.

g. Now, prepare your ice cream maker and pour the mixture into it. Follow the manufacturer's instructions for processing, which typically involves churning and freezing to transform your ingredients into a delectable frozen treat.

Did you know?

- Frodo Baggins, the central character in J.R.R. Tolkien's The Lord of the Rings, embarked on a perilous journey to destroy the One Ring. This dessert, named after him, represents the unexpected and delightful surprises that can be found along even the most challenging journeys.
- The light and fluffy texture of this dessert reflects the resilience and determination displayed by the characters in Tolkien's epic saga. Just as Frodo and his companions faced daunting obstacles, this dessert combines seemingly disparate elements to create a delightful whole.
- In the world of Middle-earth, where various cultures and races coexist, the surprise in this dessert mirrors the diverse and richly layered universe created by Tolkien. Just as the unexpected alliances and discoveries shaped the story, the layers of creamy and fluffy goodness in Frodo's Surprise offer a delightful surprise in each bite.

6. Prune Tree Cake

Fruit laden trees are found everywhere in the shire, and plums are no exception. Try this sweet treat with some crushed pecans and sauce.

Prep Time: 30 minutes

Servings –14

List of Ingredients:

- 8 oz of prunes, pits removed
- 12 oz of white sugar
- 1/2 an oz of ground allspice
- 1 teaspoon of baking soda
- 1 teaspoon of cinnamon, ground
- 1/2 teaspoon of salt
- 8 oz of vegetable oil
- 2 lightly beaten eggs
- 12 oz of pecans, chopped
- 4 oz of water
- 16 oz of all-purpose flour
- 1 teaspoon of nutmeg, ground
- 8 oz of buttermilk

Icing:

- 4 oz of buttermilk
- 1 oz of corn syrup
- 8 oz of white sugar
- 4 oz of margarine
- 1 teaspoon of vanilla extract

sssssssssssssssssssssss

Methods:

a. Begin by preheating your oven to a toasty 350 degrees Fahrenheit, getting it ready for baking this delightful Prune Tree Cake.

b. In a saucepan, place the prunes along with water over medium-high heat. Allow the mixture to come to a gentle boil. Once it's bubbling away, reduce the heat to low and let it simmer for about 5 minutes, or until the prunes become wonderfully soft. Once done, drain the prunes and set them aside.

c. Now, prepare your Bundt pan by generously greasing it and lightly dusting it with flour. This will ensure your cake doesn't stick and comes out with ease once it's baked to perfection.

d. In a mixing bowl, it's time to sift together 12 oz of sugar, allspice, flour, cinnamon, nutmeg, baking soda, and salt. This step combines all the dry ingredients and ensures they are well mixed for the perfect cake.

e. In another bowl, stir together the oil, 8 oz of buttermilk, and the eggs until they form a harmonious blend. Using an electric mixer, incorporate those softened prunes into the buttermilk mixture. Beat until the prunes are broken down into small bits. Add the pecans and stir them in for that delightful crunch.

f. Transfer your beautifully blended batter into the prepared Bundt pan, spreading it out evenly. Now, it's time to bake. Place the pan in your preheated oven and let the cake bake for about 45 minutes or until it's wonderfully set. You'll know it's done when a toothpick comes out clean.

g. While your cake is cooling in the Bundt pan for about 10 minutes, it's time to prepare a delectable icing. In a saucepan over medium-high heat, combine 8 oz of sugar, 4 oz of buttermilk, margarine, vanilla, and corn syrup. Bring this mixture to a boil and let it cook for about 5 minutes, stirring occasionally.

h. Once your cake has cooled slightly and your icing is ready, gently pour the warm icing over the cake while it's still in the Bundt pan. This step adds a sweet, gooey layer of goodness to your Prune Tree Cake.

Did you know?

- The name "Prune Tree Cake" might not sound as enchanting as some of the dishes found in Middle-earth, but it pays homage to the Shire's simple and down-to-earth cuisine. Hobbits, like Samwise Gamgee and Frodo Baggins, appreciated hearty and wholesome food, and this cake would have been a favorite among them.
- Just as the Shire is a place of warmth and camaraderie, the combination of prunes, spices, and pecans in this cake creates a comforting and harmonious flavor profile. It reflects the sense of community and togetherness seen throughout J.R.R. Tolkien's tales.
- The icing drizzled over the cake represents the sweet moments of respite and celebration in the midst of epic adventures. In Tolkien's stories, characters often found solace and joy in the simplest pleasures, much like indulging in a slice of this Prune Tree Cake.

7. The Eye of Sauron

I like to put some edible gold flakes in the middle of this Bundt cake to really create the eye of Sauron. Try this delicious cake for your second breakfast or elevenses with some hot coffee.

Prep Time: 5 minutes

Serve: 12

List of Ingredients:

- 2 oz of roasted almonds, chopped
- 2 ½ oz of erythritol
- 1 oz of coconut flour
- 6 oz of almond flour
- ½ teaspoon of vanilla extract
- 1 pinch of salt
- 6 large eggs
- 4 ½ oz of butter
- 1 oz of pumpkin pie spice
- ½ an oz of baking powder
- 2 oz of cream cheese

ssssssssssssssssssssssss

Methods:

a. To embark on the journey of making The Eye of Sauron, first, preheat your oven to a toasty 350 degrees Fahrenheit. This will ensure your creation bakes to perfection.

b. Next, prepare your Bundt baking pan by giving it a good coating of cooking spray. This step is essential to prevent your cake from sticking to the pan and to make it easier to remove later.

c. In a frying pan, melt some butter over low heat, and then sprinkle in the enticing pie spice. Allow them to meld together, infusing the butter with that delightful spicy aroma. Once done, remove the pan from the heat and let it cool down a bit.

d. In a large mixing bowl, it's time to work on the heart of your cake. Beat together eggs, vanilla, and erythritol until the mixture becomes delightfully fluffy. Then, introduce the cream cheese into this egg mixture, stirring until they come together in creamy harmony.

e. In another bowl, whisk together the almond flour, coconut flour, baking powder, and a pinch of salt. Make sure you achieve a clump-free and perfectly blended dry mixture.

f. Now, gradually add this dry mixture to your egg and cream cheese mixture, stirring diligently until you have a smooth and well-combined batter. Don't rush this step; it's all about achieving the right consistency.

g. Stir in the melted butter and pie spice mixture, making sure every bit of your creation is infused with that enticing spice flavor. Set the batter aside for a brief 1-2 minutes to allow it to meld and develop its flavors. Then, carefully pour it into the prepared Bundt pan.

h. Let the magic happen in the oven as you bake your creation on the bottom rack for approximately 31-35 minutes. Keep a close eye on it, and when a tester inserted in the center comes out clean, your Eye of Sauron is ready to shine.

i. Once removed from the oven, allow your masterpiece to cool before serving. This cooling period allows the flavors to settle, making each bite a true adventure.

Did you know?

- The Eye of Sauron is a powerful and malevolent symbol of the Dark Lord's watchful presence in J.R.R. Tolkien's Middle-earth. This dessert, bearing the same name, captures the intensity and intrigue of the series, offering a flavorful experience worthy of the epic tales.
- The combination of spices in this cake represents the diverse cultures and landscapes found in Middle-earth. Just as the characters encounter a rich variety of flavors on their journeys, The Eye of Sauron combines ingredients to create a captivating taste sensation.
- In Tolkien's world, the battle against evil often requires unity and resilience. Similarly, the intricate blending of ingredients in this recipe reflects the importance of harmony and balance, resulting in a dessert that is both captivating and delicious.

8. Lemon Ice

Where Bilbo got lemons in the Shire is a question for speculation in the chat rooms. Some say they were carried by birds while others say the market may have sold them.

Prep Time: 25 minutes

Serve: 6

List of Ingredients:

- 14 oz of heavy whipping cream
- ¼ teaspoon of yellow food coloring
- Zest and juice from 1 lemon
- 3 large eggs, nicely separated into whites and yolks
- 2 ½ oz of erythritol

sssssssssssssssssssssss

Methods:

a. To embark on creating a refreshing Lemon Ice, begin by taking your egg whites and placing them in a mixing bowl. Using an electric mixer, beat them until they reach the point where stiff peaks form. This step is crucial for achieving the light and airy texture of your dessert.

b. In a separate bowl, shift your focus to the egg yolks and erythritol. Whisk them together until they become delightfully fluffy. This mixture will add a touch of sweetness and a creamy consistency to your Lemon Ice.

c. Now, it's time to infuse your creation with that bright lemony goodness. Add a dash of food coloring and the zesty lemon juice to the yolk mixture. Gently fold in the previously beaten egg whites to combine everything harmoniously. This step marries the airy whites with the yolks, creating a well-balanced mixture.

d. In yet another mixing bowl (yes, we're getting a workout with our bowls), whip some cream until it forms peaks. Once you've achieved those peaks, fold the egg white and yolk mixture into the whipped cream. This step is all about bringing all the delightful components together.

e. With your mixture ready to shine, it's time to transfer it into an ice cream maker. Follow the manufacturer's instructions for processing, which typically involves churning and freezing to turn your ingredients into a refreshing and creamy Lemon Ice.
f. Finally, once your Lemon Ice is perfectly churned and ready, serve it up for a cool and satisfying treat. It's a delightful way to beat the heat and enjoy the bright flavors of lemon.

Did you know?

- The zesty and refreshing nature of Lemon Ice mirrors the lively and adventurous spirit of hobbits like Frodo and Bilbo Baggins in J.R.R. Tolkien's tales. Just as they embarked on epic journeys, this dessert offers a journey of flavor and refreshment.
- In Middle-earth, lemons and their refreshing qualities may not be common, but the recipe's creative use of lemon juice adds a touch of brightness reminiscent of the Shire's simple yet delightful cuisine. It's a perfect representation of the balance between simplicity and flavor found in Tolkien's works.
- The careful folding and blending of ingredients in this recipe symbolize the unity and cooperation seen among the characters in the Lord of the Rings series. Just as Frodo and his companions worked together to overcome challenges, this dessert brings together various elements to create a harmonious and delicious final product.

9. LOTR Pudding

This pumpkin spice pudding would be the perfect dessert for any LOTR Halloween party you are hosting. It would never show up in the books, though, as Tolkien was consistent in using Ancient European foods.

Prep Time: 5 minutes

Serve: 6

List of Ingredients:

- ¼ teaspoon of vanilla extract
- 4 egg yolks
- ½ a clementine
- 14 oz of heavy whipping cream
- ⅓ oz of pumpkin pie spice
- 1 oz of erythritol

sssssssssssssssssssssss

Methods:

a. To start crafting your delightful LOTR Pudding, preheat your oven to a cozy 360 degrees Fahrenheit. This will ensure the perfect baking temperature for your dessert.

b. In a small pan, set the stage by bringing the cream to a gentle boil. Now, it's time to add some enchanting flavors. Introduce the pie spice, erythritol, and a dash of vanilla into the cream, and let them mingle as you bring the mixture back up to a boil. These aromatic ingredients will infuse your dessert with warmth and sweetness.

c. Once your cream mixture is thoroughly infused and simmering with delightful flavors, remove the pan from the heat. Now, with a whisk in hand, it's time to work some magic. While constantly whisking, carefully pour the aromatic cream into the egg yolks. Keep whisking until they combine harmoniously. This step ensures a velvety-smooth texture for your pudding.

d. Prepare 6 ramekins for your individual servings. Place them in a large and deep baking dish. Now, pour the creamy mixture evenly into these ramekins, filling them up with your enchanting concoction.

e. To create a magical baking environment, pour water into the baking dish until it reaches halfway up the sides of the ramekins. This water bath will help your pudding cook gently and evenly.

f. Slide your baking dish into the preheated oven and let the pudding bake for approximately 30 minutes. Keep an eye on it, and when it's done, remove it from the heat. Allow it to cool to your desired temperature, whether you prefer it warm or chilled.

g. To add a refreshing and citrusy twist, serve your enchanting LOTR Pudding topped with clementine wedges. These wedges not only enhance the flavor but also bring a burst of vibrant color to your dessert.

Did you know?

- The Lord of the Rings series is filled with unexpected journeys and magical encounters. This LOTR Pudding captures the essence of adventure and enchantment, making it a perfect treat for fans of Tolkien's epic tales.
- Just as the characters in Tolkien's world often share simple yet heartwarming meals, this pudding represents the camaraderie and bonds formed during their adventures. It's a reminder that even in the face of darkness, there is room for joy and togetherness.
- The water bath used in the baking process symbolizes the importance of balance and teamwork in the Lord of the Rings. Just as Frodo relied on his companions, this dessert relies on the harmonious combination of ingredients and techniques to create a delicious and memorable treat.

10. Sweet Tater Cake

The scene between Gollum and Samwise discussing the best type of foods is memorable. Sam's family were known as experts in growing potatoes.

Prep Time: 20 minutes

Servings –14

List of Ingredients:

- 8 oz of softened butter
- 16 oz of white sugar
- 1 teaspoon of vanilla extract
- 4 large eggs
- 24 oz of all-purpose flour
- 1 teaspoon of cinnamon, ground
- 1/2 teaspoon of nutmeg, ground
- 1/4 teaspoon of salt
- 3/4-oz of orange juice
- 1 oz of orange zest, grated
- 16 oz of cooked sweet potatoes, mashed
- ⅓ oz of baking powder
- 1/2 teaspoon of baking soda
- 8 oz of confectioners' sugar, sifted

sssssssssssssssssssssss

Methods:

a. To create a delightful Sweet Tater Cake, let's begin by preheating your oven to a cozy 350 degrees Fahrenheit. This will ensure the perfect baking temperature for your cake.

b. Now, prepare a 10" Bundt pan for your cake. Give it a good greasing and follow up with a light dusting of flour. This will ensure your cake doesn't stick to the pan and comes out beautifully intact.

c. In a large bowl, it's time to blend the dry ingredients that will make your cake magical. Sift together the baking powder, flour, cinnamon, baking soda, a pinch of salt, and a dash of nutmeg. This step ensures that your cake batter is well-mixed and clump-free.

d. In another bowl, let's focus on the heart of your cake. Cream together the butter and granulated sugar until they form a creamy and smooth mixture.

e. Now, introduce the sweet potatoes and vanilla to this buttery concoction. Use your mixer to blend them in until they are thoroughly combined. This step adds that wonderful sweet potato flavor and a touch of warmth to your cake.

f. It's time to add the eggs, one at a time, to your mixture. Make sure to mix well before adding the next one. This gradual incorporation ensures a smooth and consistent batter.

g. With the eggs blended in, it's time to introduce the dry ingredients. Gradually beat the flour mixture into the wet ingredients until they come together seamlessly. This step brings all the elements of your cake together.

h. Transfer this beautifully blended batter into your prepared Bundt pan, spreading it out evenly. Now, let's bake this masterpiece for approximately 80 minutes, or until it's perfectly set. Keep an eye on it to ensure it's baked to perfection.

i. Once the cake is done baking, allow it to cool for 20 minutes. This short resting period prepares it for the final touch.

j. While the cake is cooling, let's prepare a delicious glaze. Mix confectioners' sugar with 2/3 ounce of orange juice in a small bowl. Adjust the sugar or orange juice to achieve the right consistency for your glaze. This glaze will add a delightful sweetness and citrusy zing to your Sweet Tater Cake.

k. To complete your masterpiece, spoon the icing generously over the cake, allowing it to flow down the sides. Garnish your creation with some vibrant orange zest, adding a burst of color and flavor.

Did you know?

- The mention of sweet potatoes in this recipe connects it to the simple yet hearty meals enjoyed by the hobbits in J.R.R. Tolkien's tales. Sweet Tater Cake embodies the spirit of hobbit cuisine, known for its comforting and wholesome dishes.
- Just as the characters in the Lord of the Rings series bond over shared meals and experiences, this cake brings people together over its delightful flavors. It's a reminder of the importance of camaraderie and connection, even in the face of adversity.
- The addition of orange zest and juice in the glaze pays homage to the vivid and colorful world of Middle-earth. Just as Tolkien's writing is known for its rich descriptions and vibrant imagery, this cake's garnish adds a visual and flavorful flourish to the dessert, making it truly enchanting.

11. Sam and Rosie Chocolate Strawberries

This dish is a sweet treat for lovers, so it is fitting that Sam and Rose would partake. The romantic chocolate dipped strawberries will have that special Hobbit in your life swooning.

Prep Time: 10 minutes

Serve: 6

List of Ingredients:

- 12 oz of chopped dark chocolate
- ½ an oz of orange zest, grated
- 1 teaspoon of Cointreau
- 10 oz of heavy cream
- 1 ½ oz of orange juice, freshly squeezed

sssssssssssssssssssssss

Methods:

a. To embark on creating these delightful Sam and Rosie Chocolate Strawberries, let's start by taking a heavy saucepan. In it, gently heat the cream and orange juice over medium heat. You'll want to keep an eye on it until the liquid begins to gently boil, infusing it with that delightful citrusy aroma.

b. Now, it's time to bring the saucepan off the heat. With the liquid still warm, whisk in the remaining ingredients from your List of Ingredients. Be diligent in your whisking, ensuring that everything combines smoothly into a luscious chocolatey fondue. This step is all about achieving a silky and sumptuous texture.

c. To keep your fondue at the perfect temperature while serving, transfer it to a fondue pot set on Low. This will ensure that your chocolate remains warm, inviting, and ready for dipping those delectable strawberries.

Did you know?

- Samwise Gamgee and Rosie Cotton, beloved characters from J.R.R. Tolkien's The Lord of the Rings, represent the enduring spirit of love and friendship amidst epic adventures. These chocolate strawberries pay tribute to their enduring bond, as they are perfect for sharing with someone special.
- Just as the characters in Tolkien's world find comfort and solace in the simple pleasures of life, like a cozy meal at home, these chocolate strawberries offer a taste of that same warmth and happiness. They are a reminder that even in the midst of great quests, it's the small moments of joy that matter most.
- The combination of chocolate and strawberries in this recipe reflects the contrast between different elements in Tolkien's stories, from the darkness of Mordor to the beauty of the Shire. Similarly, the rich chocolate fondue complements the fresh and vibrant strawberries, creating a delightful harmony of flavors and textures.

12. Helm's Deep Bundt Cake

'This cake would be the perfect offering for the large party of dwarves that came to call on Bilbo. Decorate each slice with whipped cream and strawberries.

Prep Time: 15 minutes

Servings -1

List of Ingredients:

- 8 oz of sour cream
- 2 oz of softened cream cheese
- 4 large eggs
- 16 oz of almond flour
- 4 oz of butter, diced
- 8 oz of erythritol
- 1/3-oz of baking powder
- 1 teaspoon of vanilla extract

sssssssssssssssssssssss

Methods:

a. To embark on creating this delightful Helm's Deep Bundt Cake, begin by preheating your oven to a cozy 350 degrees Fahrenheit. While it's heating up, take a moment to grease a 9" Bundt pan with butter, ensuring that your cake won't stick. Set the prepared pan aside for now.

b. In a large mixing bowl, focus on your dry ingredients. Sift together the almond flour and baking powder, ensuring a smooth and clump-free mixture. This step sets the foundation for your cake's texture.

c. In a microwave-safe bowl, it's time to blend the butter and softened cream cheese. Microwave them together for 30 seconds, and then give them a good stir to create a creamy blend.

d. Now, introduce the sweetener, vanilla extract, and sour cream into your buttery mixture. Stir these ingredients together until they create a harmonious and flavorful combination.

e. Gradually add this wet mixture to your bowl of sifted almond flour and baking powder. Stir diligently to ensure that all the components come together seamlessly. This step is all about achieving the right consistency for your cake batter.
f. With your batter well-blended, it's time to introduce the eggs. Stir them into the batter until they are fully incorporated, adding a delightful richness to your creation. Now, it's ready to be poured into the prepared Bundt pan.
g. Slide your Bundt pan into the preheated oven and let your Helm's Deep Bundt Cake bake for approximately 50 minutes. Keep an eye on it, and when a tester inserted into the center comes out clean, your cake is perfectly done.
h. Now, here's the secret to an even more delicious Helm's Deep Bundt Cake: let it cool overnight before serving. This resting period allows the flavors to meld and develop, ensuring a truly delightful experience when you finally indulge.

Did you know?

- Helm's Deep is a fortified stronghold in the Lord of the Rings, known for its resilience and strength. This cake, named after the iconic location, represents the idea that even in the face of challenges, there's room for sweetness and comfort.
- The almond flour used in this recipe reflects the resourcefulness of characters like Samwise Gamgee, who had to make do with what they had on their epic journey. Almonds were a valuable source of sustenance in Middle-earth, much like they are in this delectable cake.
- The act of cooling the cake overnight is reminiscent of the patience required on a long journey, much like the epic quest in the Lord of the Rings. Just as the characters had to wait for their efforts to bear fruit, allowing the cake to rest results in a more flavorful and satisfying dessert.

13. Lemon Butter

Frodo's discovery of lemons in the woods sparks questions about how such a tropical fruit could end up in the Shire. Spread this delicious butter on pound cake or muffins.

Prep Time: 10 minutes

Serve: 4

List of Ingredients:

- 4 oz of water
- ½ an oz of lemon juice
- ⅓ oz of butter
- 2 oz of white sugar
- ½ an oz of cornstarch
- 1/4 teaspoon of lemon zest, grated

sssssssssssssssssssssss

Methods:

a. To create the luscious Lemon Butter sauce, start by placing a saucepan over medium heat. In the pan, combine the sugar, cornstarch, and the zest of a lemon. Stir these ingredients together thoroughly. This initial step sets the foundation for your flavorful sauce.

b. Next, introduce water and freshly squeezed lemon juice into the pan. Continue to stir constantly for approximately 2-4 minutes, or until you notice the sauce thickening and starting to bubble. This step is essential for achieving that perfect, velvety texture that will make your Lemon Butter truly delightful.

c. Finally, as the sauce reaches its peak of flavor and thickness, it's time to remove it from the heat. Now, gently stir in the butter until it melts completely into the mixture. This final touch adds a rich and creamy finish to your Lemon Butter sauce.

Did you know?

- In J.R.R. Tolkien's Middle-earth, lemons are not a commonly mentioned fruit, but the use of lemon in this recipe reflects the creativity and adaptability of hobbit cuisine. Just as hobbits make the most of their local ingredients, this Lemon Butter sauce showcases the magic of combining simple elements to create something special.
- The process of carefully stirring and thickening the sauce symbolizes the patience and determination of characters in the Lord of the Rings series. As they faced trials and tribulations on their epic journey, they relied on their resilience to overcome challenges. Similarly, creating a perfect Lemon Butter sauce requires attentive stirring and persistence to achieve the desired consistency.
- Lemon Butter is a versatile addition to various dishes, providing a burst of flavor and brightness. In a way, it represents the hope and optimism that characters like Frodo and Sam carried with them, even in the darkest of times. Just as they brought light to Middle-earth, this sauce can transform a meal into something extraordinary, offering a taste of optimism and joy.

14. Lembas Biscuits

These tasty tokens make wonderful travel fare for any adventure you are heading towards. Also known as Elven Bread or Waybread in the Tolkien books.

Prep Time: 10 minutes

Serve: 18

List of Ingredients:

- 2 oz of coconut oil
- 4 egg yolks
- 8 oz of sugar-free dark chocolate chips
- 6 oz of walnuts- roughly chopped
- 2 oz of room temperature butter
- 1 oz of Stevia sweetener
- 8 oz of coconut flakes

sssssssssssssssssssssss

Methods:

a. To craft these delightful Lembas Biscuits, begin by preheating your oven to a toasty 350 degrees Fahrenheit. While it's warming up, take a moment to line your baking sheet with parchment paper. This ensures that your biscuits won't stick and makes for easy cleanup. Once that's done, set it aside for now.

b. In a large mixing bowl, let's bring together the key ingredients that will transform into your Lembas Biscuits. Combine the oil, softened butter, Swerve (a sugar substitute), and a delightful egg. Stir these ingredients until they merge into a creamy mixture.

c. Now, it's time to elevate your biscuits with some scrumptious additions. Stir in chocolate chips, coconut flakes, and chopped nuts. These ingredients not only add texture but also bring a rich and nutty flavor to your biscuits. It's the perfect blend of sweet and crunchy.

d. To shape your Lembas Biscuits, use an ice cream scoop to scoop out portions of the batter. Place these scoops onto your prepared baking sheet, ensuring they have enough space to spread and bake to perfection.

e. Slide your baking sheet into the preheated oven and let your biscuits bake for approximately 15-20 minutes. Keep a watchful eye on them until they achieve that beautiful golden brown color. This step is all about bringing out their delightful aroma and flavor.

Did you know?

- Lembas bread, also known as Elvish waybread, plays a significant role in the Lord of the Rings series. It serves as a portable and sustaining food for the characters during their arduous journeys. These Lembas Biscuits, inspired by the iconic waybread, offer a taste of the nourishment and comfort that the original Lembas provided to the characters in Middle-earth.
- The use of coconut flakes and nuts in this recipe reflects the diverse ingredients found in the world of Middle-earth. Just as Tolkien's tales feature a wide range of cultures and landscapes, these biscuits showcase a blend of flavors and textures, creating a harmonious and satisfying treat.
- Baking these biscuits with care and attention mirrors the importance of camaraderie and unity among the characters in the Lord of the Rings. Just as they relied on each other's strengths and support, the process of creating these biscuits requires the right combination of ingredients and a watchful eye to ensure they turn out perfectly, just like the fellowship in Tolkien's epic saga.

15. Aragorn's Gift

This beautiful sauce would make a wonderful addition to the Aragorn and Arwen's wedding table. Try pouring a small amount of brandy on each slice before serving.

Prep Time: 10 minutes

Serve: 8

List of Ingredients:

- 9 oz of softened unsalted butter
- 1 oz of orange juice
- 2 oz of brandy
- 16 oz of confectioners' sugar, sifted
- 1 oz of orange zest

sssssssssssssssssssssss

Methods:

a. To craft the exquisite Aragorn's Gift, begin by gathering all your essential ingredients. You'll need 9 oz of softened unsalted butter, 1 oz of orange juice, 2 oz of brandy, 16 oz of confectioners' sugar (sifted to ensure a smooth texture), and 1 oz of fragrant orange zest. With these components ready, let's move on to creating the magical sauce.

b. In a culinary symphony, place all of your ingredients into your trusty blender. The softened butter, orange juice, brandy, sifted confectioners' sugar, and the vibrant orange zest all come together in a harmonious blend. The result should be a lusciously smooth mixture, brimming with flavor.

c. Now that your sauce has been perfectly orchestrated in the blender, it's time to transfer it to a bowl. This step allows your Aragorn's Gift to take a moment to chill and solidify. Place the bowl in the refrigerator for approximately 1-2 hours, giving the sauce time to set and intensify its delightful flavors.

Did you know?

- Aragorn, a central character in J.R.R. Tolkien's The Lord of the Rings, embodies leadership, honor, and bravery. This Aragorn's Gift sauce is a symbol of generosity and the spirit of giving that permeates Tolkien's world. Just as Aragorn bestowed his gifts upon his friends and allies, this sauce adds a touch of luxury and indulgence to any dessert.
- The use of brandy and orange zest in this recipe reflects the diversity of flavors and ingredients found in Middle-earth. Just as Tolkien's world is rich and multifaceted, this sauce combines the warmth of brandy with the zest of oranges, creating a complex and delightful taste experience.
- Chilling the sauce before serving mirrors the importance of patience and anticipation in the Lord of the Rings. Just as the characters had to endure challenges and trials on their epic journey, this brief waiting period allows the flavors to meld and intensify, resulting in a sauce that's even more satisfying when it finally graces the palate.

16. Bag End Blueberry Crepe

This delectable treat would make a fine second breakfast. It is too bad that Bilbo will not be home for some time to enjoy it!

Prep Time: 5 minutes

Serve: 4

List of Ingredients:

- Whipped cream to taste
- 1 warm crepe
- ½ an oz of blueberry jam
- 8 ¾ oz of frozen blueberries
- Icing sugar for dusting

sssssssssssssssssssssss

Methods:

a. To embark on creating the delightful Bag End Blueberry Crepe, start by gently warming the crepe. Place it in the microwave for about 10 seconds, allowing it to become warm and pliable. This step ensures that your crepe is at the perfect temperature for the next stages.

b. Once your crepe is warmed, it's time to add a burst of fruity goodness. Spread ½ oz of jam evenly over the surface of the crepe. This jam will infuse the crepe with a delightful sweetness and a hint of tartness, creating a harmonious flavor.

c. Now, it's time to give your crepe its final form. Roll up the crepe, carefully enclosing the delicious jam within. This rolling action not only makes for a visually appealing presentation but also allows each bite to be a delightful combination of textures and flavors.

d. To complete your Bag End Blueberry Crepe, place it gracefully on a plate. Now, it's time to adorn it with the crowning jewels of this dessert: top it generously with fresh blueberries, a dusting of icing sugar, and a dollop of whipped cream. These finishing touches add a burst of color, sweetness, and creamy indulgence to your crepe.

Did you know?

- Bag End, the cozy hobbit hole in the Shire, is the home of Bilbo and Frodo Baggins in J.R.R. Tolkien's The Lord of the Rings. This crepe recipe pays homage to the comforting and simple delights of hobbit cuisine, which often featured fresh and wholesome ingredients like blueberries.
- Blueberries, with their vibrant blue hue and sweet-tart flavor, are reminiscent of the natural beauty and bountiful landscapes of Middle-earth. Just as the Shire is known for its lush countryside, this crepe celebrates the charm of hobbit culture and their love for fresh, homegrown produce.
- The combination of jam, blueberries, icing sugar, and whipped cream reflects the diverse flavors and treats that characters enjoyed throughout their journeys in Tolkien's world. Just as they encountered a wide range of culinary experiences, this Bag End Blueberry Crepe offers a taste of adventure and comfort, reminding us of the importance of savoring life's simple pleasures.

17. Gimli's Brownies

Much like the dwarf these are named after, these brownies are sweet, dark and a little nutty. If Gimli had a sweet tooth, these would definitely satisfy him.

Prep Time: 5 minutes

Serve: 16

List of Ingredients:

- 2 large eggs
- 1 teaspoon of vanilla extract
- 3 ½ oz of all-purpose flour
- 1 ¾ oz of butter
- 3 oz of cocoa powder, unsweetened
- 7 oz of sugar

ssssssssssssssssssssssss

Methods:

a. To embark on creating these delectable Gimli's Brownies, let's begin by melting the butter. Take a microwave-safe bowl and place the butter in it. Then, heat it in the microwave on high for about 40 seconds. This step will transform the butter into a silky, liquid form, ready to blend with the other ingredients.

b. Now, it's time to infuse your brownie mixture with sweetness and richness. Mix in the sugar, cocoa, and a touch of vanilla extract into the melted butter. Stir diligently until these ingredients meld together into a harmonious and flavorful mixture. This is the foundation of your indulgent brownies.

c. One by one, introduce the eggs into the butter mixture. Be sure to lightly beat each egg before adding the next. This step ensures that each egg is fully incorporated into the batter, contributing to the perfect texture and richness of your brownies.

d. Gradually, add the flour into the batter. Stir attentively to ensure that the flour blends seamlessly, resulting in a smooth and clump-free brownie mixture.

e. Now, prepare your brownie dish for the baking adventure. Coat a glass brownie dish with cooking spray to prevent sticking. Once the dish is well-prepared, pour the brownie batter into it evenly, creating a level surface that will bake to perfection.

f. Slide the brownie dish into the microwave and set it to high power for 4-5 minutes. This is the crucial baking phase that transforms your batter into scrumptious brownies. Keep an eye on it as it bakes to ensure it reaches the desired texture and doneness.

g. Once the brownies are out of the microwave, allow them to cool for about 10 minutes. This short resting period ensures that they hold their shape when you cut them into squares, making for perfect, satisfying portions.

Did you know?

- Gimli, a valiant dwarf from J.R.R. Tolkien's The Lord of the Rings, is known for his love of hearty and flavorful meals. These brownies capture the essence of his appreciation for the simple yet comforting pleasures of life.
- The melting process in this recipe symbolizes the forging of powerful bonds among the characters in Middle-earth. Just as the Fellowship of the Ring came together for a common purpose, the ingredients in these brownies combine to create a delightful treat.
- Enjoying these brownies is like savoring a moment of respite in the midst of an epic journey, much like the characters in Tolkien's world. They remind us that even during challenging times, there's room for sweetness and the joy of simple indulgences.

18. An Unexpected Cinnamon Cheesecake

While the Hobbits are used to having many meals every day, when Gandalf and his entourage show up at Bilbo's, his pantries are put to the test. This delicious cinnamon treat would have been well received by the dwarves in this party.

Prep Time: 15 minutes

Serve: 6

List of Ingredients:

- 1 teaspoon of vanilla extract
- ½ a teaspoon of maple extract
- 2 ½ oz of powdered erythritol
- ¼ teaspoon of ground cloves
- ¼ teaspoon of salt
- ½ teaspoon of ground cinnamon
- 1 ½ oz of butter, unsalted
- 5 large eggs, room temperature
- 6 oz of heavy whipping cream, room temperature
- 2 oz of softened cream cheese
- 1 teaspoon of baking powder
- 1 oz of unflavored whey protein isolate
- 1 teaspoon of ground ginger

Toppings

- freshly whipped heavy whipping cream
- ground cinnamon
- powdered erythritol

sssssssssssssssssssssss

Methods:

a. Begin your culinary adventure by preheating your oven to a toasty 400 degrees Fahrenheit. This step ensures your cheesecake will bake to perfection. While your oven is warming up, let's gather the essential ingredients for this delightful treat.

b. In a food processor, combine all the ingredients listed, except for the unsalted butter. This harmonious blend will form the base of your luscious cheesecake. Allow the food processor to work its magic for about 1 minute, transforming the ingredients into a smooth and velvety mixture.

c. Now, it's time to infuse your creation with a touch of sizzle and aroma. Place the unsalted butter in an oven-safe frying pan and let it heat in the oven until it begins to sizzle. This step adds a rich, buttery flavor to your cheesecake that's simply irresistible.

d. Once your sizzling butter is ready, remove it from the oven with care. Now, gently pour the mixture from the blender into the sizzling butter in the frying pan. This transfer is where the magic truly begins, as your cheesecake takes shape in the oven.

e. Return the pan to the oven and let your cheesecake bake for approximately 12-15 minutes. Keep a close eye on it; you'll know it's ready when the cake is beautifully browned and has puffed out. To ensure it's perfectly set, insert a toothpick into the center; if it comes out clean, your cheesecake is good to go.

f. Once your An Unexpected Cinnamon Cheesecake is out of the oven, you have a choice to make—serve it hot for a comforting experience or let it cool for a delightful chilled treat. Top it with freshly whipped heavy whipping cream, a sprinkle of ground cinnamon, and a dusting of powdered erythritol to complete this delicious creation.

Did you know?

- The unexpected twists and surprises in J.R.R. Tolkien's The Hobbit inspired the name "An Unexpected Cinnamon Cheesecake." Just as Bilbo Baggins' journey was filled with unforeseen adventures, this cheesecake offers unexpected layers of flavor, from the warm cinnamon to the creamy cheesecake goodness.
- Cinnamon, cloves, and ginger are key spices in this recipe, reminiscent of the diverse cultures and flavors found throughout Middle-earth. These spices symbolize the rich tapestry of Tolkien's world, where various races and lands contribute to the epic narrative.
- The choice of hot or cold serving options reflects the diverse preferences and climates of Middle-earth. Just as different regions in Tolkien's world had distinct climates and customs, this cheesecake caters to a variety of tastes, ensuring a satisfying treat for all.

19. Hadhafang Spears

In the film, Arwen holds a sword called Hadhafang and possesses great powers. These skewers also possess the power to cure your hunger.

Prep Time: 10 minutes

Serve: 6

List of Ingredients:

- ½ an oz of brewed coffee
- 1/8 teaspoon of cinnamon, ground
- 16 oz of milk chocolate chips
- 1 ½ oz of heavy cream
- 1 oz of cherry brandy

ssssssssssssssssssssssss

Methods:

a. A.To embark on crafting the enchanting Hadhafang Spears, you'll need to begin with the essential ingredients at your side. Gather together ½ an oz of brewed coffee, 1/8 teaspoon of ground cinnamon, 16 oz of delectable milk chocolate chips, 1 ½ oz of luxurious heavy cream, and 1 oz of aromatic cherry brandy. With these ingredients in hand, let's delve into creating this delightful treat.

b. In a harmonious fusion of flavors and textures, place all of the listed ingredients into a fondue pot. The brewed coffee, ground cinnamon, milk chocolate chips, heavy cream, and cherry brandy all come together in a delightful medley. These ingredients promise a journey through layers of taste sensations.

Did you know?

- Hadhafang is a sword with a rich history in J.R.R. Tolkien's legendarium. It was wielded by Arwen, an elven princess, and symbolizes her strength and determination. These Hadhafang Spears, with their blend of flavors, pay homage to Arwen's character, showcasing both elegance and strength in the realm of culinary delights.
- The addition of cherry brandy adds a touch of Middle-earth's mystique to this recipe. It's reminiscent of the diverse and intriguing beverages found in Tolkien's world, from the fine wines of Rivendell to the hearty ales of the Shire. Just as the characters in the story savor different drinks on their quests, these spears offer a unique and alluring flavor profile.
- Fondue, with its communal and interactive nature, is a fitting choice for a recipe inspired by The Lord of the Rings. The fellowship of characters in the story often shared meals and moments together, reinforcing the bonds of friendship and unity. These Hadhafang Spears bring people together, inviting them to enjoy the magic of Tolkien's world and the joy of shared experiences.

20. Spiderweb Fondue

This fondue resembles the spiderweb set as a trap for Frodo. Try this fondue with some chocolate, fruit or chunks of pound cake.

Prep Time: 20 minutes

Serve: 2

List of Ingredients:

Red Velvet Fondue

- 8 oz of light coconut milk, divided
- 7 oz of finely chopped dark chocolate (70%)
- 1 teaspoon of vanilla
- 1 small peeled beet
- ½ an oz of melted coconut oil

Cream Cheese Swirl

- 3 ½ oz of finely chopped white chocolate
- 2 oz of light coconut milk
- 3 oz of softened light cream cheese

ssssssssssssssssssssss

Methods:

a. To embark on creating the captivating Spiderweb Fondue, let's begin by preparing the beets. Place a steamer insert in a pot filled with boiling water, and steam the beets until they become tender. This gentle steaming process ensures that the beets will blend seamlessly into our delightful fondue.

b. Once the beets have reached the desired tenderness, it's time to transform them into a velvety puree. Transfer the steamed beets to a food processor and combine them with a touch of coconut oil and 2 oz of creamy coconut milk. Blend these ingredients together until they form a smooth and vibrant beet puree, which will infuse our fondue with a stunning hue and earthy flavor.

c. Now, let's turn our attention to the dark chocolate. In a Dutch oven over low heat, melt the dark chocolate until it becomes irresistibly silky. This luxurious melting process sets the stage for the decadent base of our fondue.

d. To elevate the flavor profile of our fondue, add the remaining coconut milk and a dash of vanilla to the melted dark chocolate. Gently stir these ingredients together, creating a harmonious mixture that combines the richness of chocolate with the subtle sweetness of coconut and the warmth of vanilla.

e. It's time to introduce the vibrant beet puree into the chocolate mixture. Carefully blend the beet puree with the chocolate, ensuring that the colors and flavors intertwine seamlessly. This addition not only enhances the fondue's visual appeal but also adds a unique twist to the taste that is both delightful and unexpected. Once the mixture is well-combined, remove it from the heat, ready to create our spiderweb design.

f. In a double boiler, gently melt the white chocolate over low heat. Once it's smoothly melted, set it aside to cool to room temperature. This cooled white chocolate will play a crucial role in crafting the intricate spiderweb design that will grace our fondue.

g. Now comes the artistic part. In a fondue pot, layer the dark chocolate mixture, cream cheese, and the cooled white chocolate. To create a captivating spiderweb design, use a toothpick to carefully swirl the layers together. This step not only adds a visually stunning element to our fondue but also combines the rich flavors of dark and white chocolate with the creaminess of cream cheese in a mesmerizing way.

Did you know?

- The intricate spiderweb design in this fondue pays homage to Shelob, the giant spider encountered by Frodo and Sam in J.R.R. Tolkien's The Lord of the Rings. This design captures the essence of Middle-earth, where even the smallest details can hold hidden beauty and danger.
- The addition of beets to the fondue represents the earthy and natural elements of Tolkien's world. The author's deep connection to nature is reflected in the descriptions of lush landscapes and the importance of preserving the environment, making the use of beets a fitting tribute to his themes.
- Fondue, with its communal and interactive nature, mirrors the fellowship and bonds formed by the characters in the story. Just as the characters shared meals and experiences on their journey, this Spiderweb Fondue encourages people to come together and enjoy the magic of Tolkien's world while savoring the flavors of Middle-earth.

21. Middle Earth Coconut Balls

Serve these delicious bite-sized treats with your favorite LOTR cocktail or a hot cup of tea. Indeed, you will be amazed at how easy these are to eat with a thick, grey beard.

Prep Time: 10 minutes

Servings -16

List of Ingredients:

- 3-5 drops of vanilla creme
- 1/2 teaspoon of vanilla
- 1 pinch of pink salt
- 5 ½ oz of almond butter
- 2 ½ oz of coconut flour
- 2 navel oranges, zested
- 2 oz of orange juice

sssssssssssssssssssssss

Methods:

a. Let's embark on a journey to create Middle Earth Coconut Balls, a delightful treat inspired by the enchanting world of J.R.R. Tolkien. To begin this culinary adventure, gather your ingredients and follow these steps:

b. In a large mixing bowl, combine the harmonious blend of butter, 2 oz of flour, the vibrant zest of an orange, the refreshing juice of an orange, the creamy essence of vanilla crème, the fragrant allure of vanilla extract, and a pinch of pink salt. Stir this wondrous mixture until all the ingredients unite into a delightful, aromatic dough.

c. Now, let's shape our creation into delectable balls. Using an ice cream scoop, portion out equal-sized balls of the dough. Then, take these doughy treasures into your hands and gently smooth them, ensuring they are perfectly round and enticing.

d. To add a delightful outer layer of coconut goodness, roll each ball in the remaining coconut flour. This step not only enhances the flavor but also provides a delightful contrast in texture.

e. Lay your freshly coated coconut balls on a baking sheet lined with parchment paper. This will ensure they stay intact and maintain their shape during chilling.

f. Finally, let your Middle Earth Coconut Balls rest and chill for about 10-20 minutes. This step allows the flavors to meld together and the coconut coating to set, resulting in the perfect balance of flavors and textures.

Did you know?

- The enchanting flavors of orange zest and juice in these coconut balls are reminiscent of the vibrant and diverse landscapes of Middle-earth. From the lush forests of Lothlórien to the arid deserts of Harad, J.R.R. Tolkien's world is a tapestry of natural wonders, and the citrusy notes in this recipe celebrate the variety of flavors found in the fictional realm.

- Coconut, a key ingredient in this recipe, symbolizes the resilience and resourcefulness of the characters in The Lord of the Rings. Just as the hobbits, elves, and other inhabitants of Middle-earth displayed adaptability in the face of adversity, the use of coconut in these balls reflects the creativity and innovation of Tolkien's characters.

- The act of shaping and rolling these coconut balls mirrors the unity and camaraderie that the fellowship of characters in the story shares. Just as the characters joined together on their quest, these balls represent a harmonious blend of ingredients coming together to create a delightful treat.

22. Sam's Squares

The only way for any character in the Tolkien is in rice pudding, but these squares make certainly a nice addition to a party table. Arrange these in a jagged formation with an edible Gollum at the top.

Prep Time: 30 minutes

Serve: 32

List of Ingredients:

- 3 oz of Rice Krispies cereal
- 8 ½ oz of chocolate chips
- 4 Mars Bars
- 6 oz of butter, divided

sssssssssssssssssssssss

Methods:

a. Begin by preparing the chocolatey base for your squares. Place the chocolate bars and 4 oz of butter in a microwave-safe bowl. To ensure a smooth and velvety texture, melt the mixture in the microwave in 30-second increments. After each increment, give it a gentle stir. Continue this process until the chocolate and butter are completely melted, creating a rich and indulgent chocolate sauce.

b. With the chocolate and butter melted to perfection, it's time to introduce the cereal. Add the cereal into the bowl with the melted chocolate. Gently mix these ingredients together, ensuring that every piece of cereal is thoroughly coated in the luscious chocolatey goodness. This step creates the foundation of your Sam's Squares, combining the crispiness of cereal with the decadence of chocolate.

c. Now, let's shape this delightful mixture. Press the cereal and chocolate mixture evenly into an 11"x17" baking tin. Use a spatula or the back of a spoon to firmly pack the mixture, creating a uniform and compact layer in the tin. This step sets the stage for the next layer of chocolaty goodness.

d. In another microwave-safe bowl, it's time to create the final layer of irresistible chocolate. Combine the chocolate chips and the remaining butter. Just like before, melt this mixture in 30-second increments in the microwave, stirring after each interval. This ensures that the chocolate chips and butter meld together into a silky, pourable consistency.

e. Once the chocolate chip mixture is completely melted and smooth, pour it generously over the cereal and chocolate base in the tin. This layer of chocolate chip goodness crowns your Sam's Squares with a delectable finishing touch.

f. With all the layers in place, it's time to let your creation chill and set. Place the tin in the refrigerator for a well-deserved rest of 2 hours. This chilling process allows the layers to firm up, ensuring that each square holds its shape perfectly.

g. After the squares have chilled to perfection, it's time to cut them into delectable portions. Slice the chilled creation into squares of your desired size, and savor the delightful combination of crispy cereal and velvety chocolate in each bite.

Did you know?

- Samwise Gamgee, one of the beloved characters in The Lord of the Rings, is known for his unwavering loyalty and love for his friends. These Sam's Squares, with their layers of chocolate and cereal, symbolize the layers of friendship and devotion found in the story, just as Sam was always there to support Frodo and his fellow hobbits.

- The combination of chocolate and cereal in this recipe reflects the diverse and unexpected flavors found in the rich tapestry of Middle-earth. From the simple joys of hobbit meals to the elaborate feasts of elves and men, Tolkien's world is filled with culinary delights, making these squares a fitting tribute to the gastronomic wonders of his imagination.

- The act of sharing and cutting these squares into equal portions mirrors the camaraderie and unity that the fellowship of characters in The Lord of the Rings shared on their epic journey. Just as they relied on one another, these squares bring people together, inviting them to savor the magic of Tolkien's world while enjoying a sweet treat with friends and loved ones.

23. Gandalf's Coffee Cake

If Bilbo had access to these **List of Ingredients:** when Gandalf showed up at his house with a pack of dwarves, this would have made a perfect dessert. Serve with some tea or coffee as a sweet end to a meal.

Prep Time: 30 minutes

Servings –12

List of Ingredients:

Coffee Cake:

- 1 teaspoon of vanilla extract
- 8 oz of sour cream
- 24 oz of all-purpose flour
- 1 teaspoon of baking powder
- ½ an oz of cinnamon, ground
- 2 oz of white sugar
- 6 oz of softened butter
- 12 oz of white sugar
- 3 large eggs
- 1 teaspoon of baking soda
- 4 oz of walnuts, chopped

ssssssssssssssssssssssss

Methods:

a. Begin by preheating your oven to 400 degrees Fahrenheit, setting the stage for the magical baking adventure ahead.
b. Prepare a 10" Bundt pan by generously coating it with cooking spray, ensuring that your cake will release effortlessly once it's baked to perfection.
c. Now, let's dive into the heart of this recipe by creating the cake batter. In a mixing bowl, using an electric mixer, beat together the butter and 12 oz of sugar until a fluffy, peak-like consistency forms. This step infuses the batter with a rich and buttery texture.

d. One by one, add the eggs to the buttery mixture, making sure to combine each egg thoroughly before introducing the next. This gradual addition ensures a smooth and uniform incorporation.

e. To enrich the flavor profile, introduce a touch of enchantment with the addition of vanilla extract. Mix it into the batter until it melds seamlessly with the other ingredients.

f. In a separate bowl, combine the baking soda, baking powder, and flour. Sift these dry ingredients together, creating a harmonious blend that will add structure and lightness to your cake.

g. Gradually, begin adding the sifted flour mixture to the wet batter, alternating with dollops of sour cream. Stir well between each addition, creating a luscious, well-balanced batter that is both flavorful and moist.

h. To add a delightful crunch and nutty aroma, gently fold walnuts into the batter, ensuring they are evenly distributed throughout the mixture.

i. Now, it's time to assemble your coffee cake. Transfer half of the prepared batter into the greased Bundt pan, spreading it evenly across the bottom.

j. In a separate bowl, combine 2 oz of sugar and fragrant cinnamon, creating a sweet and spicy blend. Sprinkle this mixture evenly over the layer of batter in the pan, introducing a layer of delightful cinnamon-sugar swirl.

k. To complete the assembly, add the remaining batter in mounds on top of the cinnamon-sugar layer, using your hands or a spoon to create an enticing, layered effect.

l. With all the components in place, it's time to bake your coffee cake. Begin by baking it at 400 degrees Fahrenheit for an initial 8 minutes. Then, reduce the oven temperature to 350 degrees Fahrenheit and continue baking for an additional 40 minutes or until the cake is beautifully set and golden brown.

Did you know?

- Gandalf, the wise wizard of Middle-earth, often shared his wisdom and guidance with the Fellowship of the Ring on their epic quest. Similarly, this coffee cake brings together a harmonious blend of flavors and textures, just as Gandalf united the diverse characters of Middle-earth to achieve a common goal.
- The combination of cinnamon and sugar in this recipe reflects the comforting and homey flavors found in hobbit cuisine. The hobbits, known for their love of simple and hearty meals, would surely appreciate the warm and inviting aroma of this coffee cake.
- The magical swirls created by the layering of batter and cinnamon-sugar in this cake mirror the intertwining destinies and adventures of the characters in The Lord of the Rings. Each bite is a delightful journey through layers of flavor, just as the story takes readers on a captivating journey through the richly imagined world of Middle-earth.

24. Lord of the Ring Cake

The caramel sauce on this decadent cake is sweet and addictive. Serve this cake with some whipped cream and fresh raspberries.

Prep Time: 25 minutes

Servings –12

List of Ingredients:

- 1 teaspoon of baking soda
- 1 teaspoon of baking powder
- 5 ¼ oz of softened butter, divided
- 1 large egg
- 1 oz of strong brewed coffee
- 8 oz of whole milk
- 2 oz of Cajeta, Mexican caramel sauce
- 12 oz of all-purpose flour
- 3 oz of cocoa powder, unsweetened
- 8 oz of white sugar

Flan:

- 4 large eggs
- 1 teaspoon of vanilla extract
- 20 oz of evaporated milk
- 14 oz of sweetened condensed milk

sssssssssssssssssssssss

Methods:

a. Start by preheating your oven to a magical 350 degrees Fahrenheit, setting the stage for a delightful baking journey.

b. Coat a 9" Bundt pan with a touch of cooking spray and a light dusting of flour, ensuring your cake will release effortlessly after baking.

c. Create a water bath to add moisture to your cake's environment. Place a shallow baking pan large enough to accommodate the Bundt pan in your oven and fill it with water, ensuring it reaches about one-third of the way up the Bundt pan. Warm the water in the oven as it preheats.

d. In a microwavable bowl, place the caramel sauce and heat it for about 1 minute or until it becomes soft enough to pour. Carefully pour the caramel into the Bundt pan, ensuring that the bottom is completely covered.

e. In a separate bowl, sift together the cocoa, flour, baking soda, and baking powder. Set this dry mixture aside for now.

f. In another bowl, beat 5 ¼ oz of butter with an electric mixer until it becomes delightfully fluffy. Gradually add sugar to the mix, beating until it's fully incorporated into a harmonious blend.

g. Add one egg and coffee to the buttery mixture, and beat until the ingredients are well combined, creating a luscious and aromatic batter.

h. Transfer this flavorful batter into the Bundt pan, pouring it gently over the layer of caramel, creating a tantalizing base for your cake.

i. Now, for an extra touch of indulgence, pour the cake batter evenly over the caramel layer, ensuring a consistent and delectable distribution.

j. In a food processor, blend together evaporated milk, condensed milk, vanilla, and 4 eggs until the mixture achieves a smooth and velvety texture. To ensure a silky result, pass this milk mixture through a sieve before pouring it gently over the cake batter in the Bundt pan.

k. Place the Bundt pan into the prepared baking pan filled with warm water, and let the magic happen in the oven for approximately 1 hour, or until your cake is beautifully set.
l. Finally, let your cake cool for about 1 hour before carefully removing it from the pan, unveiling a cake worthy of Middle-earth feasts.

Did you know?

- The caramel layer at the base of this cake symbolizes the depths of adventure and discovery in Middle-earth. Just as the fellowship delved into unknown territories, your taste buds will explore the rich layers of this dessert.
- The use of coffee in the cake batter pays homage to the comforting moments shared over mugs of coffee or tea in the Shire, where hobbits cherished the simple pleasures of life.
- The water bath technique used in this recipe mirrors the importance of water throughout the journey in The Lord of the Rings. Whether it's crossing rivers or replenishing their supplies, water played a crucial role in the fellowship's travels.

25. Rosie's Butter Pecan Cheesecake

Rosie bubbly personality and maternal qualities make her the best source of delicious desserts. Fresh butter and pecans adorn this decadent cake you will definitely want the seconds of.

Prep Time: 10 minutes

Serve: 4

List of Ingredients:

Cheesecake crust

- ½ an oz of melted salted butter
- 2 oz of finely crushed pecans
- ¼ oz of powdered erythritol

Filling

- 2 oz of powdered stevia
- 1 teaspoon of vanilla extract
- Pecans
- 8 oz of softened cream cheese
- 1 oz of heavy whipping cream
- 2 oz of butter
- 1 beaten egg

ssssssssssssssssssssssss

Methods:

a. Begin your culinary journey by preheating your oven to a toasty 350 degrees Fahrenheit, setting the stage for the creation of this delightful cheesecake.

b. Take a 4-inch springform baking pan and either coat it generously with cooking spray or grease it with a touch of butter, ensuring that your cheesecake will release with ease after baking.

c. Now, in a small mixing bowl, combine the melted butter, pecans, and powdered stevia. Stir this mixture thoroughly until all the elements are well incorporated, creating a flavorful crust for your cheesecake.

d. Transfer this scrumptious crust mixture into the prepared springform pan, and with gentle yet firm pressure, press it down evenly to line the bottom of the pan.

e. Slide the pan into the preheated oven and let the crust bake for a tantalizing 6-7 minutes, allowing it to firm up and become golden brown.

f. While your crust is pre-baking, take a small saucepan and place it over medium-high heat. Melt the butter in the saucepan, stirring it until it reaches a foamy, delightful state. Be cautious not to let it burn.

g. While the crust is still warm, pour this foamy, melted butter over it, enhancing the flavors and aroma of your cheesecake crust. Allow the crust to cool as you proceed with the next steps.

h. In a medium mixing bowl, gather all the ingredients needed for the filling, excluding the pecans. With the assistance of an electric mixer, blend these ingredients until they form a smooth and creamy cheesecake filling.

i. Gradually introduce the melted butter into the filling mixture while continuing to stir, ensuring that it integrates harmoniously with the other ingredients.

j. Pour this delectable filling into the springform pan, spreading it evenly over the buttery pecan crust. Loosely tent the pan with foil, allowing steam to escape during baking.

k. The time has come to bake your cheesecake masterpiece. Place it in the oven and let it bake for 30-35 minutes, or until the cake is gloriously set.

l. Once your cheesecake has achieved the desired level of perfection, remove it from the oven and let it cool to room temperature. Afterward, transfer it to the refrigerator to chill for 2-4 hours, or better yet, overnight.

Did you know?

- Butter pecan, a prominent flavor in this cheesecake, symbolizes the cozy comforts of the Shire, where hobbits relished the simple pleasures of life and the delicious treats created by Rosie Cotton.
- The meticulous process of combining and baking the ingredients mirrors the careful planning and cooperation required among the members of the fellowship during their epic journey through Middle-earth.
- Rosie's Butter Pecan Cheesecake is a testament to the enduring sense of community and friendship that is central to The Lord of the Rings. Just as Rosie cared for the well-being of her fellow hobbits, this dessert brings people together to share in its delightful flavors.

26. Glazed Eye of Sauron

Serve this Bundt cake with some edible gold candies in the center to make it look like the actual eye. This dessert tastes amazing with some fruit on the side and a little bit of whipped cream.

Prep Time: 30 minutes

Servings –14

List of Ingredients:

- 1/2 teaspoon of baking soda
- 8 oz of butter
- 4 oz of vegetable shortening
- 8 oz of white sugar
- 4 mashed ripened bananas
- 5 large eggs
- 2 oz of milk
- 8 oz of pecans, chopped
- 4 oz of butter
- 2 oz of white sugar
- 1 teaspoon of vanilla extract
- 2 oz of heavy cream
- 24 oz of all-purpose flour
- 1 teaspoon of salt
- 1/2 teaspoon of baking powder
- 16 oz of brown sugar
- ⅓ oz of vanilla extract
- 2 oz of brown sugar

sssssssssssssssssssssss

Methods:

a. Begin by preheating your oven to a temperature of 325 degrees Fahrenheit. This will provide the ideal baking environment for your Eye of Sauron cake.

b. Take a 10-inch Bundt pan and generously coat it with cooking spray. Ensure that every nook and cranny is covered to prevent any sticking. Lightly dust the pan with flour to create a non-stick surface.

c. In a large bowl, using an electric mixer, beat together 8 oz of butter, shortening, 16 oz of brown sugar, and 8 oz of white sugar until the mixture becomes delightfully fluffy. This step sets the foundation for your decadent cake.

d. Now, it's time to incorporate the key ingredients that will infuse your cake with flavor. Add ripe bananas and eggs to the butter mixture alternately, ensuring that each addition is well incorporated. The final touch is a dash of 1/3 oz of vanilla extract to enhance the aroma and taste.

e. Gradually introduce the flour and milk into the batter, alternating between them and mixing thoroughly each time. This process ensures a consistent and smooth cake batter. Once the batter is ready, transfer it to your prepared Bundt pan.

f. Slide the Bundt pan into the preheated oven and let your cake bake for approximately 80 minutes or until it achieves a beautifully set texture. This step brings your creation one step closer to becoming the Eye of Sauron.

g. While your cake is baking, it's time to prepare the delectable glaze. In a pan over medium heat, combine 4 oz of butter, 2 oz of brown sugar, 2 oz of white sugar, 1 teaspoon of vanilla extract, and heavy cream. Stir diligently until the sugar dissolves completely. Let it simmer for an additional minute, allowing the flavors to meld together.

h. Once your cake has completed its time in the oven, it's still warm and inviting. While it's still in the pan, generously pour the warm glaze over the cake, letting it seep into every crevice. This step adds a rich, sweet element to your creation.

i. After glazing, give your cake a brief 10-minute respite to cool and absorb all the delectable flavors. This time will also help the cake set further.

Did you know?

- The Eye of Sauron, a symbol of power and malevolence in Middle-earth, inspired the concept behind this cake. Its intricate design and dark glaze pay homage to the ominous presence of the Dark Lord.
- The alternating additions of ingredients in this recipe reflect the harmony that the members of the Fellowship of the Ring had to achieve in order to succeed on their perilous journey to destroy the One Ring.
- Just as the Eye of Sauron cast its gaze upon Middle-earth, this cake captures the attention and admiration of all who indulge in its deliciousness, making it a delightful addition to any Lord of the Rings-themed gathering.

27. Frodo's Lemon Cakes

The Hobbits hold amazing feasts with lots of delicious English fare, and a cake made with lemons and sugar would have been enjoyed by all. Serve this with some hot coffee, tea or an aperitif.

Prep Time: 30 minutes

Servings –12

List of Ingredients:

- 3 large eggs
- 20 oz of all-purpose flour, sifted
- 1/2 teaspoon of salt
- 1 teaspoon of baking powder
- 8 oz of buttermilk
- 4 oz of golden raisins
- 2 ½ oz of white sugar
- 1 1/2 tablespoons of water
- 1 oz of fresh lemon juice
- 5 oz of butter
- 12 oz of white sugar
- ½ an oz of lemon zest, grated
- 1/2 teaspoon of baking soda
- 3/4 teaspoon of lemon extract
- 2 ½ oz of butter

ssssssssssssssssssssssss

Methods:

a. Start by preheating your oven to a toasty 325 degrees Fahrenheit, creating the perfect environment for baking these exquisite lemon cakes.

b. Take a 10-inch Bundt pan, your trusted baking companion, and give it a gentle coating of cooking spray. Lightly dust it with flour to ensure your cakes will release effortlessly once they're baked to perfection.

c. Armed with an electric mixer, embark on the first step of crafting these lemony delights. Cream together 5 oz of butter and 12 oz of sugar until the mixture reaches a state of fluffy perfection, adorned with tempting peaks that hint at the deliciousness to come.

d. Introduce the eggs one at a time into your butter and sugar mixture, ensuring thorough incorporation before adding the next. Gently fold in the lemon zest, infusing your batter with vibrant citrus notes that will tantalize your taste buds.

e. In a separate bowl, sift together the flour, baking soda, salt, and baking powder, setting the stage for a harmonious blending of dry and wet ingredients. Begin the delicate dance by alternating additions of buttermilk and the sifted flour mixture into the buttery embrace. Mix thoroughly between each addition, ensuring a perfectly blended batter.

f. Infuse your creation with even more lemony goodness by stirring in the lemon extract and plump raisins. These ingredients add layers of flavor and texture that will make your lemon cakes truly special.

g. With your batter skillfully prepared, transfer it into the awaiting Bundt pan. Spread it out evenly, ensuring a uniform bake.

h. Slide the Bundt pan into your preheated oven and let the magic happen for approximately 50 minutes, or until your lemon cakes reach a delightful level of firmness. As they bake, your kitchen will be filled with the tantalizing aroma of lemon and butter.

i. Once your cakes are baked to perfection, remove them from the oven and allow them to cool for a tantalizing 10 minutes. This period of rest allows the flavors to settle and meld together, ensuring the best possible taste.

j. As your lemon cakes cool, take 2 ½ oz of sugar, 2 ½ oz of butter, and water in a pan over medium-low heat. Watch as the butter melts and the sugar dissolves, forming a glossy glaze that will crown your lemon cakes with a sweet and tangy finish. Stir in lemon juice, enhancing the glaze with a burst of citrusy brightness.

Did you know?

- The Shire's Culinary Tradition: Hobbits in The Shire are renowned for their love of good food. Frodo's Lemon Cakes are reminiscent of the delightful treats that hobbits might enjoy during their second breakfasts or elevenses in the peaceful countryside of the Shire.
- Citrus in Middle-earth: While lemon trees aren't explicitly mentioned in J.R.R. Tolkien's works, the addition of lemon zest and lemon extract in this recipe offers a refreshing twist on traditional hobbit fare. Citrus flavors evoke the essence of adventure and discovery, just as Frodo embarked on his epic quest to destroy the One Ring.
- The Fellowship of Flavors: The careful combination of ingredients and the meticulous blending in this recipe symbolize the unity and camaraderie of the Fellowship of the Ring. Just as the members of the Fellowship brought their unique strengths together to achieve a common goal, these ingredients harmonize to create a delightful dessert.

28. Weary Traveler Buns

When you are actually on the road, and your stomach starts growling, these buns will give you a boost to finish the trek. Try them with some jelly for a nice change of taste.

Prep Time: 10 minutes

Serve: 8

List of Ingredients:

- 1 pinch of salt
- ½ teaspoon of baking soda
- 2 oz of erythritol
- 8 oz of Feta cheese, crumbled
- 1 oz of ground psyllium husk powder
- 8 oz of fine ground almond flour
- 16 oz of coconut oil
- 1 pinch of ground nutmeg
- 2 large eggs
- 4 oz of softened cream cheese

sssssssssssssssssssssss

Methods:

a. Start by heating some oil in a medium frying pan over medium heat. This will be the welcoming sizzle for our flavorful buns.

b. In a large mixing bowl, whisk together the flour, psyllium husk, nutmeg, salt, baking soda, and erythritol. This blend of ingredients will serve as the base for our buns.

c. Break the feta cheese into crumbles and mix it into the flour mixture. This addition will infuse the buns with a rich and savory taste.

d. Now, it's time to introduce the cream cheese and eggs into the mix. Gently fold them into the flour mixture until all the ingredients are beautifully combined. This step brings the dough together, ensuring a hearty and satisfying texture.

e. To test if the oil is ready for our buns, insert a wooden spoon into it. When the spoon sizzles upon contact, it's time to proceed. The sizzle signals the perfect temperature for frying.

f. Shape the dough into 8-10 balls, ready to be transformed into delightful buns. Drop them one by one into the sizzling oil with care and attention.

g. Cook each bun for approximately 2-3 minutes per side, or until they achieve a uniform and tempting golden brown hue. A slotted spatula or spoon will be your trusty tools for flipping them over in the pan.

h. Once the buns have reached their golden perfection, gently lift them from the pan and allow any excess oil to drain away by placing them on a wire rack. This step not only ensures a delectable texture but also keeps the buns from being overly greasy.

i. Now, all that's left to do is let the buns cool to your desired warmth and then serve them up. They are perfect for replenishing the energy of weary travelers on a Middle-earth adventure.

Did you know?

- The Hobbit's Journey: In J.R.R. Tolkien's "The Hobbit," Bilbo and the company of dwarves embarked on a long and adventurous journey. These Weary Traveler Buns would have been a welcome sight during their travels, providing sustenance and comfort on the road.
- Hobbiton Fare: Hobbits are known for their love of good food and hearty meals. These buns, with their rich and savory flavors, capture the essence of the simple yet delicious fare found in the Shire.
- Fuel for the Quest: Just as Frodo and his companions needed nourishment for their perilous quest to Mount Doom, these buns are designed to provide travelers with the sustenance and energy needed for their own journeys and adventures.

29. Good Weather in the Shire Apple Bake

In the Shire, Bilbo would have baked this delicious sweet in the oven, but we have decided to put our own modern touches. Use your microwave for cooking this yummy treat in minutes.

Prep Time: 5 minutes

Serve: 4

List of Ingredients:

- 2 oz of all-purpose flour
- 1 ¾ oz of shredded coconut
- 4 oz of dark brown sugar
- 1/2 teaspoon of cinnamon
- 21 oz of apple pie filling
- 1 ¾ oz of butter
- 2 oz of porridge oats

sssssssssssssssssssssss

Methods:

a. Start by arranging a layer of fresh apple slices along the bottom of a microwave-safe 7" pie plate. This will be the delicious foundation of our apple bake.

b. Take a moment to melt some butter. Pop it into your microwave and set it on high for about 40 seconds until it turns into a luscious, golden liquid.

c. In a separate bowl, combine a delightful mix of oats, flour, coconut, sugar, and a dash of cinnamon. These ingredients will form a delightful crumble topping for our apple bake.

d. Pour the melted butter over this crumbly mixture and give it a good stir. You'll see the ingredients coming together to form a flavorful and aromatic crumble.

e. Now, take this crumble mixture and generously spread it over the waiting apple slices in the pie plate. Make sure it covers the apples evenly, promising a delectable crunch in every bite.

f. It's time to let the microwave work its magic. Set it to high and let the apple bake cook for 5 minutes. This will soften the apples and allow the crumble to turn into a golden, crispy delight.

g. Once the microwave timer chimes, exercise some patience and let your creation sit for another 5 minutes. This brief waiting period helps the flavors meld and the dessert settle into its deliciousness.

h. Finally, your Good Weather in the Shire Apple Bake is ready to serve. The combination of warm, tender apples and the sweet, crunchy crumble will transport your taste buds to the idyllic fields of the Shire.

Did you know?

- A Hobbit's Delight: The Shire, home to hobbits like Bilbo and Frodo Baggins, is known for its abundance of apple orchards. This recipe pays homage to the Shire's love for apples, making it a perfect treat for hobbits and fans of The Lord of the Rings.
- Simple Pleasures: Much like the hobbits' appreciation for the simple joys of life, this apple bake combines basic ingredients to create a comforting and wholesome dessert.
- Celebrating Good Weather: In The Lord of the Rings, the hobbits of the Shire often celebrate good weather with outdoor feasts and gatherings. This apple bake could easily be a part of such a celebration, symbolizing the warm and joyful spirit of the Shire's inhabitants.

30. Travel Party Rice Pudding

Make sure when you travel you bring all your pots and pans like Samwell. He is the one companion who prepares to cook up a gourmet meal on a moment's notice.

Prep Time: 5 minutes

Serve: 2

List of Ingredients:

- 2 oz of raisins
- a pinch of ground nutmeg
- 54 ½ oz of cooked rice
- 1 beaten egg
- 8 ¾ oz of milk
- a dash of vanilla extract
- 2 oz of sugar

ssssssssssssssssssssssss

Methods:

a. Start by gathering all the ingredients needed for this delightful Travel Party Rice Pudding. Having everything ready will make the process smoother.
b. In a microwave-safe bowl, combine the cooked rice, sugar, raisins, and a pinch of ground nutmeg. These ingredients will create the base of your delicious rice pudding.
c. In a separate container, beat the egg until it's well-mixed and ready to add a delightful richness to the pudding.
d. Pour the beaten egg into the bowl with the rice mixture. This will help create a creamy texture as the pudding cooks.
e. Gradually add the milk to the mixture. Stir it in carefully, ensuring that all the ingredients are well combined.
f. Now, it's time to add a dash of vanilla extract. This will infuse the pudding with a delightful aroma and flavor that will transport your taste buds.
g. Stir the entire mixture thoroughly, making sure the ingredients are evenly distributed.

h. With all the ingredients well combined, it's time to let the microwave do its work. Cook the mixture on high for 2 minutes, allowing the flavors to meld and the pudding to start taking shape.

i. After the initial 2 minutes, switch the microwave to a low setting and continue cooking for an additional 8 minutes. Be sure to stir the pudding every 2 minutes to prevent any unwanted lumps from forming.

j. Once the timer goes off and your rice pudding is cooked to perfection, remove it from the microwave. Allow it to cool for about 5 minutes before serving.

Did you know?

- A Portable Treat: Rice pudding is a convenient and portable dessert, making it an ideal choice for a travel party. In J.R.R. Tolkien's Middle-earth, characters often embark on epic journeys, and a dish like this would be a delightful addition to their provisions.
- Comfort in a Bowl: Rice pudding is known for its comforting and homey qualities. Much like the comfort of a warm hearth in the Shire, this dessert brings a sense of coziness and familiarity to any gathering.
- A Sweet Reward: Just as characters in The Lord of the Rings find solace and respite in moments of camaraderie and simple pleasures, this rice pudding can be a sweet reward after a long day of adventures.

31. Spider's Eyes Brownie

Those bright black eyes of Shelob gleamed like these chocolate chips when they focused on Frodo. Thank goodness Sam saved the day, although I am sure he would much rather be eating this.

Prep Time: 10 minutes

Serve: 8

List of Ingredients:

- 2 eggs
- 4 oz of all-purpose flour
- 3 ½ oz of chocolate chips
- Icing sugar for dusting
- 5 oz of butter
- 6 ¾ oz of sugar
- 2 oz of unsweetened cocoa powder
- 1 teaspoon of vanilla extract

ssssssssssssssssssssssss

Methods:

a. Begin by preparing all the necessary ingredients to ensure a smooth and efficient cooking process.

b. In a microwave-safe bowl, place a suitable amount of butter and heat it on high for about 30 seconds. The goal is to melt the butter, so keep an eye on it to avoid overheating.

c. Once the butter has melted, it's time to infuse it with sweetness. Start by pouring sugar into the bowl, followed by cocoa powder. Finish this delightful trio with a dash of vanilla extract. Mix these ingredients together thoroughly until you have a well-combined, chocolaty mixture.

d. As the mixture begins to take shape, it's time to introduce the eggs one at a time. Carefully stir in each egg before adding the next, ensuring that they are fully incorporated into the batter.

e. With the eggs well blended into the mixture, it's time to introduce the flour. Gradually add the flour and chocolate chips to the batter, combining them thoroughly. This step will result in a rich and gooey brownie consistency.

f. Prepare an 8-cup silicone tray by evenly dividing the brownie batter among the cups. Silicone trays are great for easy removal and portioning.

g. Place the tray in the microwave and cook on high for approximately 2 minutes. Keep a close watch during this time to prevent overcooking.

h. Once the brownies are done, carefully remove the tray from the microwave. Let them cool in the cups for about 10 minutes. This resting period allows the brownies to set and become the perfect treat.

i. To add a finishing touch of sweetness, dust the brownies with icing sugar before serving. This step not only enhances the flavor but also gives them an inviting appearance.

Did you know?

- Mirkwood Forest Inspiration: The name "Spider's Eyes Brownie" evokes the eerie spiders of Mirkwood Forest in J.R.R. Tolkien's Middle-earth. Just as our heroes faced these arachnids, you can conquer these delicious brownies with courage.
- Hobbit Comfort Food: Brownies are known for their comforting and indulgent nature, much like the cozy and wholesome meals enjoyed by hobbits in the Shire. This recipe combines modern sweetness with a touch of that rustic charm.
- Sweet Quest Rewards: In The Lord of the Rings, characters embark on epic quests and face countless challenges. Just as they find moments of rest and solace in the midst of their adventures, these Spider's Eyes Brownies can be a delightful reward after a day of your own journeying.

32. Elvish Nut Brittle

When Legolas speaks of the elves, he mentions their talents and superiority. This nut brittle would have made a wonderful treat for his traveling party.

Prep Time: 10 minutes

Serve: 6

List of Ingredients:

- 8 oz of popped popcorn
- 8 oz of dry-roasted peanuts
- 1 oz of butter
- 1 teaspoon of baking soda
- 1/3 oz of vanilla extract
- 8 oz of sugar
- 4 oz of light corn syrup
- 1/8 teaspoon of salt

sssssssssssssssssssssss

Methods:

a. To begin crafting this delightful Elvish Nut Brittle, first, prepare a 15"x10" jellyroll pan by greasing it. This will ensure that your brittle doesn't stick and will be easy to remove once it's set.

b. In a glass bowl, combine the enchanting trio of corn syrup, sugar, and a pinch of salt. Stir these magical ingredients together until they are well-mixed and ready to embark on their culinary journey.

c. Place the glass bowl in the microwave and heat the mixture on high for approximately 5 minutes. Keep a watchful eye to ensure it doesn't overflow, as sugar can be quite playful when heated.

d. Once the syrupy concoction has spent its time in the microwave, it's time to introduce the hearty peanuts. Stir them into the bubbling syrup mixture, and return the bowl to the microwave.

e. Continue the enchantment for another 2-4 minutes, or until the peanuts take on a glorious golden brown hue. This step infuses the nuts with a rich, toasty flavor that will make your brittle truly exceptional.

f. With your creation reaching its final stages, quickly stir in the butter, baking soda, and a touch of vanilla extract. This is where the magic truly happens, as the buttery, aromatic essence of vanilla melds with the other ingredients.

g. Now, it's time to pour this enchanting mixture into the prepared jellyroll pan. Once it's all in, give the pan a gentle shake to help settle the ingredients into an even layer.

h. The final touch of the spell involves patience. Allow the brittle to cool and set naturally. During this time, it will transform into a crisp and delightful treat.

Did you know?

- Elvish Elegance: The name "Elvish Nut Brittle" pays homage to the grace and sophistication of the Elves in J.R.R. Tolkien's world. Just as the Elves bring an aura of mystique to Middle-earth, this brittle infuses your kitchen with its own enchantment.
- Nuts from the Shire: Peanuts, a key ingredient in this recipe, are reminiscent of the simple and nourishing foods cherished by the hobbits of the Shire. Despite their humble origin, these nuts can be transformed into a delightful, Elvish-inspired delicacy.
- Breaking of the Fellowship: As you break the cooled brittle into pieces, it's a symbolic reminder of the trials and separations faced by the Fellowship of the Ring during their epic journey. Enjoy the shared experience of savoring this brittle together, much like the companionship of the characters in Tolkien's epic tale.

Author's Afterthoughts

Let me just say thank you! But I don't want to bore you to death with a bunch of stuff and make this seem like a love letter. While I am very grateful for your support, I see you as more of a friend than a reader. And as my friend, I'd like to be an even better friend so that we can continue to spend many more days in the kitchen together!

This is where I ask, what kind of recipes would you like to see from me? I may not be standing right next to you every time you turn on the oven or be there to help you wash dishes but trust me when I say I'm there at heart. It couldn't be any other way when I pour my heart and soul into my recipes! You might just see a picture-perfect dessert or appetizer, but behind it lie countless failed attempts and overcooked versions of the same dish. My neighbors and friends also test all of my recipes about 10 times before deciding on the final recipe…Each recipe within my books is more special than you know.

Not everything is about me, though. As a cookbook writer and friend, I'd like to know what your pantry staples are, what ingredients you cook with the most, how much time you spend in the kitchen per week, etc. I want to know it all! Knowing this can give my future recipes purpose. I can design them to specifically meet specific needs like family dinners on a budget, simple vegan breakfasts, avocado recipes, and more. I may be the one developing the recipes, but don't forget you're whom I make recipes for! So, help a sister out?

Love,

Mia Martin

Made in United States
Orlando, FL
22 February 2025